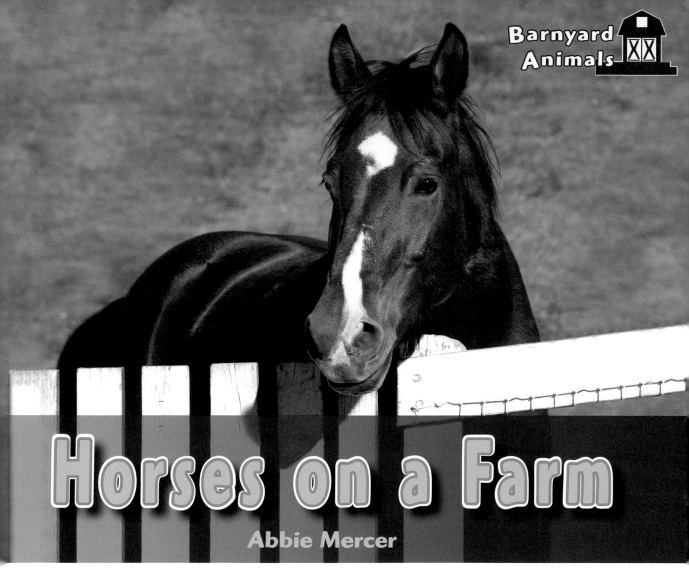

Horses on a Farm

Abbie Mercer

PowerKiDS press.

New York

For Katie Keating

Published in 2010 by The Rosen Publishing Group, Inc.
29 East 21st Street, New York, NY 10010

First Edition

Editor: Amelie von Zumbusch
Book Design: Kate Laczynski
Photo Researcher: Jessica Gerweck

Photo Credits: All images from Shutterstock.

Library of Congress Cataloging-in-Publication Data
Mercer, Abbie.
  Horses on a farm / Abbie Mercer. — 1st ed.
      p. cm. — (Barnyard animals)
  Includes index.
  ISBN 978-1-4042-8052-6 (library binding) — ISBN 978-1-4042-8065-6 (pbk.) —
ISBN 978-1-4042-8066-3 (6-pack)
  1. Horses—Juvenile literature. I. Title. II. Series.
  SF302.M47 2010
  636.1—dc22
                                        2008050338

Manufactured in the United States of America

Contents

Horses are beautiful and powerful animals. They can run very fast.

Horses live on farms. Horses need lots of room to run around.

Horses live in stables, or barns. Each horse in a stable has its own **stall**.

Many kids visit farms to ride horses.
Riding a horse is lots of fun!

Every horse has a **mane** and a tail.
Horses also have **hooves**.

13

Horses can be many different colors. Black, gray, and **bay** are some horse colors.

There are several breeds, or kinds, of horses. This horse is an Arabian.

Horses eat mostly grass and hay. They need to drink clean water, too.

19

Baby horses are known as foals. Foals can stand within hours of being born!

Foals drink their mothers' milk and grow quickly. Young horses like to run and play.

Words to Know

bay

hooves

mane

stall

Index

Web Sites

Due to the changing nature of Internet links, PowerKids Press has developed an online list of Web sites related to the subject of this book. This site is updated regularly. Please use this link to access the list:
www.powerkidslinks.com/byard/horses/